ESSEX

Gho

Prepare to be frightened

BRADWELL
BOOKS

Published by Bradwell Books
9 Orgreave Close Sheffield S13 9NP
Email: books@bradwellbooks.co.uk

British Library Cataloguing in Publication Data: a catalogue
record for this book is available from the British Library.

1st Edition
ISBN: 9781909914087

Print: Gomer Press, Llandysul, Ceredigion SA44 4JL
Design by: jenksdesign@yahoo.co.uk

Photograph Credits: ShutterStock and credited individually
front cover ShutterStock/Sue Chillingworth

CONTENTS

Layer Marney Tower
Layer Marney Tower is undoubtedly Essex's most spectacular haunted house.
© James Parker

INTRODUCTION

The former kingdom of the East Saxons can lay claim to being England's oldest county. It is certainly one of the most historic. Colchester is England's oldest recorded town, starting in the Iron Age before the Roman invasion as Camelodunum. Colchester's medieval castle is possessed of the largest keep in Europe and was partly constructed from the ruins of a Roman temple. The county town of Chelmsford was founded by the Romans in about the year AD60. It was granted city status in 2012.

Essex boasts a wealth of beautiful villages and towns, many with more than their share of medieval houses. There are more than 14,000 listed buildings in the county, over a thousand of which have won Grade I status.

Essex also has an extraordinarily rich folklore. With its extensive marshes and winding inlets of the sea and the Thames, large swathes of this eastern county remained isolated for centuries, developing a character and dialect all their own. In these odd corners old beliefs and superstitions died hard. In the 17th century, the county proved a lucrative base of operations for the self-styled Witchfinder General, Matthew Hopkins, one of the most notorious state-approved serial killers in history. Even into the 19th century, there flourished so called 'cunning men' – individuals supposedly skilled in magic and blessed with second sight who acted as unofficial doctors and policemen in their isolated communities.

Echoes of these dark times are echoed in the ghost-lore of Essex: the hideous 'familiar' said to haunt the notorious Devil's House on Wallasea, for example, or the presence of a suspected witch murdered by a mob in Finchingfield. The ghosts of Essex are many and varied and date from all periods of its turbulent history. Roman centurions rub ghostly shoulders with medieval monks and nuns, Tudor lords and ladies, Civil War and Second World War soldiers, and numerous anonymous spooks. Some are quiet ghosts, others noisy. One or two are surprisingly violent, grotesque and frightening. All are fascinating. Not so long ago, Essex was even able to lay claim to Britain's 'most haunted house': the infamous Borley Rectory.

Special mention must be made of James Wentworth Day, for it is a name we will encounter often in this book. Wentworth Day (1899-1983) was born in Suffolk but lived most of his adult life in Essex. A lover of the land and a particularly keen wildfowler, Wentworth Day spent many years befriending the country folk of East Anglia and in this way discovered many Essex-based ghost stories, including first-hand encounters that would otherwise have been lost to obscurity. Many of these tales were repeated in the several books of ghost stories he published in his lifetime, particularly *Ghosts and Witches* (1954), *A Ghost Hunter's Game Book* (1958) and *Essex Ghosts* (1973).

—

HAUNTED HOUSES

Essex can lay claim to a number of celebrated haunted homes, including England's 'most haunted', as examined in the following chapter.

Springfield Place is a handsome mansion in the north-east part of **Chelmsford**. Springfield was a separate village for centuries, and still remains a separate parish, but has now been swallowed up by 19th and 20th century expansion. A Springfield villager, William Pynchon, was an early settler in the Americas and the towns of Springfield in Massachusetts and Idaho are both named after his former home (by extension, so may many of the other Springfields throughout the USA, including the home town of cartoon family *The Simpsons*!).

For many years Springfield Place had a haunted reputation. Just after the Second World War, when the house was used as accommodation for young women employed at a nearby factory, the *Essex Weekly News* reported that an outbreak of 'strange happenings' was giving the occupants sleepless nights. It would seem mild poltergeist activity had broken out in the house (there is a reference to 'things falling') but the most serious disturbance was that girls sleeping on the top floor were waking up terrified because 'something uncanny had touched their faces'. The girls were moved to another part of the house and were then able to sleep in peace.

Following the publication of this report, the newspaper received a letter from Mary Petre, whose grandparents had lived in Springfield Place and experienced a number of uncanny events of their own. The Petres had taken up residence in 1864 and they soon came to realise that a large bedroom known as the Blue Room was haunted. Nevertheless, one night in 1868, the Petres' eldest daughter Lucy decided to move into the Blue Room because her baby was teething and restless and she did not want to disturb her husband's sleep. Giving the baby some rusks to chew on, Lucy began to doze off, but was then awoken by the child chuckling and talking to herself. 'Funny man, funny man!' she was saying.

Lucy looked up and was startled to see, standing in front of the fireplace, his arms folded and gazing at mother and child, 'a hideous little man'. Lucy was so terrified that in a moment of pure instinct she covered her head with the bedclothes.

Springfield Place in Chelmsford had a haunted reputation for many years.
Creative Commons

Re-emerging, she saw that the 'little man' had vanished from the room. The baby continued her 'funny man' chatter, however. The apparition was never seen again, but only because no one dared to sleep in the Blue Room again.

Springfield Place is a private home and so too is Rochford Hall at **Rochford** (Essex has remarkably few haunted 'show homes' compared to other counties). Rochford Hall dates back to the 13th century, with extensions and improvements carried out over the subsequent centuries. During the Tudor period the house was owned by Anne Boleyn's father, Thomas. Anne Boleyn is one of England's busiest ghosts: she crops up in a number of different houses, including her childhood home Hever Castle in Kent; Blickling Hall in Norfolk; the Merchants' House in Southampton; and the Tower of London, where the unfortunate young woman had her life cut tragically short by the executioner's axe. The girl who would become Henry VIII's second wife would have spent a great deal of time at Rochford Hall and some believe it was here that she first met the fickle king.

Bearing in mind her romantic popularity and her prevalence for haunting other places associated with her life, it's no wonder that the female phantom reported from Rochford Hall has also been optimistically identified as that of Anne Boleyn. Some of the witnesses to this quietly haunting ghost say that she appeared to be headless, thereby confirming for many that this is indeed Anne's shade. Antony Hippisley-Coxe, in his *Haunted Britain*, states that the ghost tends to walk on the twelve nights following Christmas.

Hippisley-Coxe mentions two more haunted houses that don't seem to have been highlighted by other authors. He writes, under the heading of **Cold Norton**: 'In a house called De Laches is a bedroom which no animal will enter. At 2am appears a small woman in Victorian dress, whom the owners describe as the epitome of evil.' He also states that Edwin's Hall, near **Woodham Ferrers**, is haunted by a Cavalier and a girl who drowned in the lake.

13th century Rochford Hall is haunted by a ghostly woman who may be Henry VIII's ill-fated second wife Anne Boleyn.
Reproduced by courtesy of the Essex Record Office

Carmel King refers to a dramatic haunting at The Tudor House, **Maldon**. In her *Haunted Essex*, she recounts a story of jealous love between two sisters. One of the girls stole her older sister's lover and then married him. It must have been gall and wormwood for the jilted woman to live in the same house as the man she had loved and her treacherous sibling. Eventually the simmering resentment boiled over and the older woman suffocated her sister with a pillow as she slept in her bed. The murderess continued to live on in the house, a tormented woman wracked with guilt.

It is the murderer rather than the victim who haunted the house. The apparition was described as a wretched-looking woman with 'straggly grey hair' who would be seen staring out of an upstairs room. A priest who attempted to speak to the spirit found himself being pushed away by an invisible force. For years the house was disturbed by mysterious thumps and crashes and the servants were said to have been 'terrorised' by the ghost. All is quiet today, however.

Another unpleasant haunting is recounted by Joan Forman in her *Haunted East Anglia*. Soon after moving into a cottage in the hamlet of Catmere End near **Saffron Walden**, the Willis family noticed a strong smell of smoke about the place. The aroma would come and go quite inexplicably. They also became aware of a feeling of unease in the rooms at one end of the cottage. They would hear the sound of children's feet running along the passage outside their bedroom, but always found their own little boy tucked up in bed. Their four-year-old then gave them the creeps by chattering about the 'woman wearing funny clothes' (a long skirt and a large hat) who sometimes visited him at night, crying her eyes out.

In addition to the smell of smoke, a revolting stench was also detected from time to time in the garden near the study window at the 'bad' end of the house. One day their son told them he had seen 'his lady' digging in the garden at this spot. On another he said he could see a crowd of people staring at the house from a nearby hedge, with some sort of 'engine' behind them. Most upsetting of all, the little boy reported seeing the faces of children staring at him, their eyes bulging and their tongues 'hanging out'.

The Willises later learnt that their cottage had experienced a fatal fire in the middle of the 19th century, in which several children died. That perhaps explained the smell of smoke and possibly the 'engine' and the crowd. The other phenomena were less easily explained and the Willises decided they'd rather not investigate further. They moved out. Having quitted the premises, they returned on just one occasion, to check everything was tidy. On this occasion, despite the fact that it had been locked and empty for several days, Mrs Willis found that the fireplace in an upstairs room had been laid with wood and kindling. Who had done it? Did the fatal fire start in this room? More mysteries!

Of the houses that are open to the public, one of the grandest is certainly Audley End House, which is also situated near Saffron Walden. At the end of a drive there stands an entranceway called the Lion Gate, after the stone lion which surmounts it. A spectral coach and horses with a headless coachman has been seen emerging from the Lion Gate. It then sets off on an unearthly trundle through the countryside. In addition, an eerie 'green hand' has allegedly been seen floating near the same gateway.

A phantom carriage haunts one of the gateways into Audley End House.
Shutterstock/Radek Sturgolewski

The Tower at **Layer Marney**, south of Colchester, is arguably even more magnificent than Audley End. Layer Marney Tower was built in 1520 and boasts the tallest Tudor gatehouse in Britain. This spectacular structure affords fantastic views of the surrounding countryside, down to the River Blackwater. Its gardens have been awarded Grade 2 listing status and include an original Tudor Knot Garden. Henry VIII and Elizabeth I both stayed here. The ghost of Layer Marney Tower, however, is said to be of Henry, the First Lord Marney. Henry died in 1523 before he saw the completion of his splendid home, which may be why his spirit feels the need to keep an eye on it now.

Ingatestone Hall, **Ingatestone**, is also open to the public. It was built in the 16th century by Sir William Petre, whose

*Handsome Ingatestone Manor, haunted by two notables of
the Elizabethan period*
Creative Commons

descendants lived at Springfield Place, described above. Sir
William was one of the architects of the Dissolution of the
Monasteries under Henry VIII (a nunnery originally stood
on the site of the manor house) and he continued to be a
trusted adviser to numerous monarchs, including the Roman
Catholic Mary I. Good Queen Bess stayed here in 1561. Sir
William is believed to be one of the ghosts of Ingatestone
Manor. The other is of an elegant woman in Elizabethan
costume tentatively identified as Lady Katherine Grey, sister
to the ill-fated Lady Jane.

When Valentines Mansion was constructed in 1696, it stood
in its own parkland surrounded by fields. Its pleasant gardens
and a remnant of the park have been preserved but the fields
have been steadily built over by the suburbs of **Ilford**.
Valentines Mansion ceased to be a private dwelling in 1912,
since when it has had a number of uses, including a home for
First World War refugees, a hospital and council offices. After

Two human tragedies associated with Valentines Mansion
may have led to its being haunted.
Shutterstock/ Chris Harvey

standing empty for fifteen years, the local council, using Heritage Lottery money and the goodwill of numerous volunteers, has restored the house to its former glory. Touring exhibitions and educational workshops are a particular feature of Valentines Mansion.

There are persistent rumours that Valentines Mansion is haunted. David Scanlan and Paul Robins, authors of *Paranormal Essex*, learnt of two possible ghosts from one of the volunteers. She told them the spirit of Clementina Ingleby, who lived in the mansion in the 1860s, may still linger here. Clementina was left an invalid of 'unsound mind' after an operation. The distressing sound of crying infants might be the ghost of a tragedy believed to have occurred in the 1920s, when a woman suffocated her newly born twins in a fit of depression.

THE MOST HAUNTED HOUSE?

Essex can only just lay claim to what became known as 'The Most Haunted House In England', for the village where it stood, **Borley**, lies right on the Suffolk border. The paranormal activity at Borley Rectory was first highlighted by Harry Price in a series of newspaper articles and then two books which were published in 1940 and 1946. At the time Price was Britain's best known ghost-hunter and his investigations into the phenomena at Borley Rectory became his most celebrated investigation (although accusations of self-aggrandisement and economy with the truth have since dogged his reputation).

Borley Rectory was built in the 1860s, a vast, rambling and unlovely edifice, for the Rev H. D. E. Bull. Veteran paranormal investigator Peter Underwood sums up the place well: 'Borley Rectory, as a haunted house, had everything: it was a gaunt, ugly, isolated monstrosity approached by a winding, lonely, overshadowed country lane. The red-brick house had a window bricked up here, a wing added there, and the whole impression was grotesque and ominous.'

Long before Harry Price came on the scene, a considerable amount of ghostly goings-on had been recorded by the Rev Bull and his family, and by his son, the Rev Harry Bull. Legend had it that the Rectory was built on or near the site of an ancient monastery, where a monk and nun had the misfortune to fall in love: the monk was hanged for this breach of his vows and the nun was walled up alive. History does not support the legend but when the apparition of a woman in a long gown and with a sorrowful face began to be seen about the grounds, she soon became known as 'the Nun'.

'The Nun' became the most persistent and best-known ghost of Borley Rectory, but there were others. When the house was taken over by Mr and Mrs Smith in the 1920s, they found it to be exceedingly haunted. Eerie footsteps, mysterious bangs, disembodied voices, ringing bells and strange illuminations were experienced throughout the house and Mrs Smith saw a phantom coach-and-horses standing in the courtyard. It was the Smiths who called in Harry Price. In 1930, the Smiths quitted the house and the Rev Foyster and his wife Marianne moved in. Now the haunting entered its 'classic' status.

The Nun made regular appearances in the garden, on a footpath near the house and between the house and the village church. Numerous independent witnesses owned up to seeing apparitions and experiencing a range of weirder phenomena, including stones falling out of thin air and bottles being thrown by invisible hands. On occasions such phenomena were witnessed by several observers.

Most intriguingly, messages were found scrawled on the wall or on pieces of paper left around the house. They seemed to be asking for 'light', 'prayers' and 'Mass'. Was this the Nun attempting to communicate? Attempts were made to contact the troubled spirit through séances and the planchette, with indifferent results. Questions left on a wall where writing had appeared were found to have been answered overnight, although the 'replies' were largely indecipherable.

Borley Rectory
Paranormal activity became so extreme at Borley Rectory that it became known as 'the most haunted house in England'.

Further alleged spirit communications, this time from a 'Joseph Glanvill', appeared to urge Price and his fellow investigators to dig up the cellar. This they did, and uncovered the skull of a woman. The skull showed that its owner had been suffering from a painful abscess in her jaw. Was this the Nun's skull and if so was her toothache the reason her ghost always looked so miserable? The skull was reburied with due ceremony in Borley churchyard.

By the time the skull was discovered, Borley Rectory had been abandoned and Harry Price took a year-long lease out on the property so that he could investigate it further. He and a number of other investigators stayed in the house in the hope of experiencing the ghostly phenomena for themselves.

Price set down the results of his ten years' research into the Rectory hauntings in his books *The Most Haunted House in England* and its sequel, *The End of Borley Rectory*.

Paranormal activity at the Rectory was still reported after it had been left empty. A painter who set up her easel one summer's day in the overgrown garden was startled by the sudden appearance of a huge black insect with big hypnotic eyes. It seemed to emerge out of a mist and then made straight for her face. The artist struck out at the 'Borley Bug' (as it has become known) and it fell to grass, but could not afterwards be found. A correspondent of Essex-based author J Wentworth Day's reported an encounter with a huge ghostly cat in the empty house. In February 1939 Borley Rectory was gutted by an unexplained fire. A 'spirit communication' received shortly before had apparently warned against fire. The empty rectory had become a focus for curiosity seekers by this time and the blaze may have been caused by trespassers.

Even as a ruin, Borley Rectory continued to surprise. On his visit to the gutted house, Harry Price took a number of photographs, one of which appeared to show a brick hovering in mid-air. The ruins continued to be visited by thrill-seekers but were eventually flattened. Ghosts, however, continue to be seen at Borley. Although the Nun might still occasionally manifest on the lane past the Rectory's former location, a much better bet is the village churchyard. Because of the Rectory's fame, Borley's church has rather been overlooked by ghost-hunters but has a long history of hauntings and ghost may still be seen there.

A man employed to cut the grass in the graveyard saw the apparition of the Nun (or that of a totally different nun) in broad daylight. She was standing near the hedge and although her costume was rather unusual – he described it as being black but with a gold-coloured bodice – he had no reason to believe she wasn't a real person. She appeared to be waiting for someone and, since it was rather a windy day, the witness approached the woman to suggest she shelter in the porch. But she melted away before his eyes.

Another odd phenomenon reported from the churchyard is a strong smell of incense which several people have encountered on the path leading to the south door. One woman described it as a 'sickly, clinging smell, heavy and musty'. It is confined to a small area even when a strong breeze is blowing. Disembodied footsteps have also been heard approaching the south door by people both inside and outside the church and the door has been locked or unlocked, or the latch been made to rattle, by invisible hands. Inside Borley Church – which unusually doesn't seem to have a dedication – the spooky sound of ghostly organ music has often been heard, as have strange tapping noises, often quite loud. Many years ago coffins in the crypt were found to have been mysteriously moved about. Some think the imposing monument to the Waldegrave family is the source of the ghostly goings-on, with several people reporting 'feelings of cold and unease' in its vicinity.

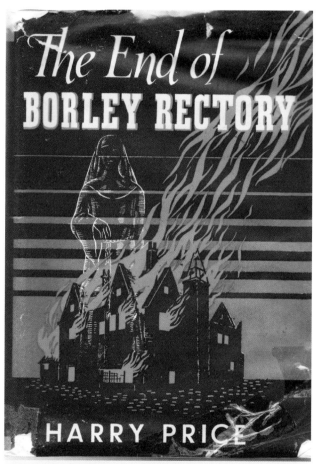

BorleyBook
The author's copy of Harry Price's The End of Borley Rectory, which detailed
the later investigations into the famous haunted house just before and after it was
mysteriously gutted by fire.

A HAUNTED CHAPEL

Many of the haunted locations in Essex are to be found on its margins, out in the marshes along its coastline. For years one of the most isolated and therefore one of the spookiest was the tiny and almost impossibly ancient chapel of St Peter's On The Wall at **Bradwell-on-Sea**. The church was founded in the 7th century by St Cedd, a Northumbrian missionary who sailed down the east coast in search of Saxons to convert to Christianity. He built the church with masonry from a ruined Roman fortress.

St Peter's is a remarkably rare survival and indeed has only just survived. It has been bashed about and patched up again numerous times down the centuries. In some ways its isolation saved it: it was never replaced by a newer church and ended up being used by local farmers, who found it a handy shelter for their animals or somewhere to store hay or equipment. A big arch in one side of the chapel shows where a hole was unceremoniously knocked through in order to allow the storage of a wagon. This has since been filled in. For many years there have been reports of a mysterious light being glimpsed through the chapel's tiny windows at night, moving about. Some of those who have investigated have also seen the light throwing into relief a number of shadowy figures. As soon as the door is opened, however, the interior is found to be in darkness. When I visited a few years ago, I found St Peter's had a tranquil and welcoming atmosphere but others have reported feeling 'a malevolent presence' within it, although this only seems to be after dark (when, these days, visitors would not be welcome and the chapel is kept securely locked).

*The Saxon chapel of St Peter's On The Wall near Bradwell-on-Sea
has a spooky reputation.*
Shutterstock/Sue Chillingworth

The area around St Peter's On The Wall also has a haunted reputation. An invisible horse has been heard galloping hell-for-leather down an old Roman track leading to the site of the Roman fort from the direction of Mersea Island. The thundering hooves tend to be heard on bright, moonlit nights and are thought to be the ghostly echo of a Roman soldier riding to the fort from the long lost Mersea watchtower. Perhaps he had spotted approaching ships and rode to warn the garrison of impending trouble.

Two-hundred yards down the shoreline from St Peter's Chapel is a former coastguard's wooden bungalow, which has been used as an observatory by Essex Birdwatching Society since 1956. Its previous owner was a wildfowler who hated birdwatchers. He called them 'weekend gull-worriers'. Ironically, his own name was Linnett. In the early 1960s, a ghost began to bother the ornithologists sleeping in the bungalow. Robert Knowles, an employee at the British Museum, was one of those startled by the apparition.

He recalled: 'It was moonlight. A man was looking through the window. He had a big nose, a mournful expression and wore a seaman's jacket with a double row of buttons. I was just going to call out to him when he seemed to float through the window and, in an instant was in the room not a yard from my face. Then I saw to my horror that there was no man at all from the waist downwards, just a misty haze, a blur.'

Mr Knowles called out to his sleeping colleague but the ghost 'immediately floated out of the room'. 'There was enough light in the room for me to see the upper half of a man perfectly plainly,' continued Mr Knowles, 'and even to see the dog shaking with fright.'

On one notable occasion a falconer woke up shivering with cold on what had been a warm, muggy night. He felt a presence in the room and was then hit on the jaw by someone or something unseen. The author James Wentworth Day, who knew Mr Linnett well, commented that he found it 'perfectly feasible that the spirit of the old fowler should return to vent his wrath upon the disturbers of his old home and shooting ground'.

The Roman road leading to 7th century St Peter's Chapel, which is believed to stand on the foundations of a gateway into a long since demolished Roman fort. Several ghosts, including one believed to date from Roman times, haunt the vicinity of the ancient chapel.

A GHOSTLY EMBRACE

One of the more unusual ghost stories from Essex focuses on the village of **Langenhoe**, in particular its now demolished church. For more than twenty years after becoming rector in 1937, the Rev Ernest Merryweather, experienced a range of strange phenomena in his church. Peter Underwood described the place as 'certainly the most haunted church I have come across'. Underwood was so intrigued by the case that he met with Mr Merryweather and was presented with a diary which detailed all the ghostly goings-on.

The first odd event took place on September 20, 1937. Mr Merryweather notes: 'It was a quiet autumn day. I was standing alone in the church, and the big west door was open. Suddenly it crashed to with such force that the whole building seemed to shake. Doors don't unusually slam to as if an express-train had hit them, when there is no palpable reason.'

The spook also enjoyed creating thumps and bumps and making objects appear or disappear. It had a particular interest in flowers: on several occasions the arrangers would find the blooms scattered or displaced within moments of them temporarily turning their backs.

Things became weirder in 1947 after Mr Merryweather paid a visit to the neighbouring manor house. He was being shown over the house when the owner mentioned that a bedroom they had just passed was never used because it was considered 'uncanny'. Intrigued, Mr Merryweather entered the room and then paused to admire the charming view to be had from its window. He had just turned away, intending to follow his hostess, who had moved on, when he was suddenly overwhelmed by the 'unmistakable embrace of a naked young woman'. For just a few seconds he felt the soft arms, breasts and body pressed against him in a 'wild and frantic' manner and then the sensation ceased.

A year passed before the rector again felt the presence of the feminine ghost. This time, she was less gentle with him. Mr Merryweather was in the church, which had recently become the victim of a repeated outbreak of vandalism, and he was so nervous at the prospect of encountering any ruffians who may have been hanging about that he had taken with him an ornamental dagger for protection. The presence of this weapon in church seems to have offended the ghost. It was snatched from his belt as he stood at the altar and at the same time he heard a female voice cry out: 'You are a cruel man.'

In 1950 the apparition of a young woman dressed in a long white gown and 'flowing headgear' began to materialise in the church and Mr Merryweather presumed this to be the lady who on two occasions had made her presence so palpably known. At about this time he was told a local legend about a woman murdered by an earlier rector who had become her lover, and he guessed this might have explained the psychic connection with himself. The ghost only ceased to manifest when the church was pulled down in 1959.

*Langenhoe Church, which became haunted by an angry female ghost in the 1940s.
The church was demolished in 1959.*
Creative Commons

MORE HAUNTED CHURCHES

The village of **Canewdon** has long had a tradition of witchcraft. The church of St Nicholas stands on one of the highest hills in Essex, overlooking the River Crouch. Like so many places in this fascinating county, the village was formerly remote and cut off, which certainly helped foster its legendary status. According to tradition, six witches will live in Canewdon so long as the church tower stands. Conversely, should the tower fall, the witches will die – an unusual link between the power of the Christian church and those who some might have considered anti-Christian or at least pre-Christian.

The last so-called 'Master of Witches' was George Pickingill. Pickingill, the son of a blacksmith, was known as a 'Cunning Man'. He carried out a reasonably lucrative trade of casting fortunes, drafting spells, curing simple ailments and generally keeping his neighbours in a state of awe.

Canewdon's reputation as 'Witch Country' has made it the focus of unwanted attention off and on since the 1970s. Even in recent years crowds of thrill-seekers or troublemakers have turned up at the church on Hallowe'en nights, although what they're expecting to happen seems uncertain. Their presence has at times been such a nuisance that police officers have been posted to keep people away. During my time as editor of *Paranormal Magazine*, I received an interesting letter from a former police officer who, one Hallowe'en night, had been tasked with patrolling the churchyard at Canewdon with a colleague. He wrote:

'One of the main reasons for being there was to stop the yobbery from entering the churchyard and causing problems, which we had managed without any trouble at all; in fact the whole evening had gone without any hitches or any major problem.'

Then something peculiar happened.

'As we walked towards the front of the church I clearly saw a young female figure walking towards the left hand side of the church. (I say walk – on hindsight, glide might be a better description). She was dressed in a long flowing light-coloured gown and had long hair. Her appearance seemed strange as it was a particularly cold evening and she seemed oddly out of place.

'My colleague also saw her and we split up to try and catch her. I ran to the left and he ran to the right of the church to stop her if she attempted to run away from me. As I ran the few yards to the side of the church I realised that she had vanished, and at this point my colleague came running round from the back of the church. "Where did she go?" I asked him. "Not past me, mate!" he replied.

'All the time I had watched her until her disappearance. When we checked, the only place she could have gone was through a doorway into the church, a large double-doored arched doorway, but this was securely locked with a large, old rusty padlock. At this point I had not considered her being a ghost but was more annoyed that someone had beaten our cordon. We checked to see if she could have hidden inside the door's recess but this was only about three inches deep. A further search revealed nothing and we carried on as normal. It was only afterwards that the realization of what we had seen hit us!'

Had they seen the ghost of one of the infamous Canewdon witches, they wondered?

The spirit of a witch buried at a nearby crossroads is said to rise out of the ground at midnight and make its way down to the river. Two other ghostly women have previously been reported from St Nicholas's churchyard, however. One is described as wearing a blue gown and may be the same apparition as that seen by the police officers. The other wears an old-fashioned poke bonnet inside which there appears to be no face.

A number of female phantoms are said to haunt the churchyard at Canewdon.
© Richard Holland

A phantom monk haunts the Church of the Holy Cross in **Basildon**. According to Andrew Green, in his *Our Haunted Kingdom*, the ghost's 'regular appearances are well established'. He continues: 'It is seen floating across the road from the graveyard and vanishes at a spot about five-hundred yards from the old church.' Witnesses have noted that the monk's robes are of an unusual 'reddish' colour. Further details have been added by Wesley Downes in his *Memories of an Essex Ghosthunter*. Downes spoke to a witness who nearly ran into the ghost with his bicycle. The apparition continued across the road and vanished on the north side of the churchyard. Downes states that the monk has also been seen floating down a footpath leading to the graveyard and one occasion in the church itself, enshrouded in a sort of mist.

According to Andrew Green, local tradition has it that the ghost is of a monk who was murdered in the 16th century, but any other clues to his identity are absent. Green also notes that a further phenomenon has been reported from the Church of the Holy Cross. 'Peculiar noises and footsteps have been heard to come from inside the 600 year old porchway of the church when it is empty at night,' he writes. Wesley Downes's *Memories* features many interesting reports personally experienced or told to the author by witnesses. He notes that in the graveyard of St John the Baptist's Church at **Great Clacton**, the apparition of a little boy has been seen in daylight running around among the headstones. He is dressed in the style of a bygone age, in knickerbockers and a 'granddad' shirt. He vanishes into thin air whenever anyone approaches him. Mr Downes has also collected a report of a ghostly choir being heard inside St Mary's Church, **Lawford**. The singing was heard one night emanating from the church, which was brightly illuminated from within. When someone went to investigate, however, the singing ceased as soon as the door was unlocked and the lights went out. The church was found to be eerily empty and silent.

Perhaps the strangest report from a haunted graveyard collected by Mr Downes is that from St Mary the Virgin Church, **Layer Marney**. This brick-built Tudor church is of a piece with the impressive Layer Marney Tower next door and was originally for the private use of the Marney family. There are rumours that Henry, First Lord Marney, haunts the church as well as the Tower but the sighting in its graveyard was very much stranger. He writes:

'In the early 1990s Mrs Sheila Charrington, who owns the estate with her husband, told me a strange story. A few Christmases earlier, they had invited a few house-guests for the holiday period and, as was their usual practice on the Christmas morning, they walked along the private path through the churchyard from the Tower to the church. To the surprise of all of them, they saw what could best be described as a spectral headless chicken running about between the gravestones, only to vanish as suddenly as it had appeared!'

Beeleigh Abbey, near **Maldon**, started life as a 12th century monastic house for the White Canons (or Premonstratensian order). Today it is a beautiful old house with celebrated gardens that are open to the public. On the Dissolution of the Monasteries, Henry VIII gave the abbey to Sir John Gate, who set about turning it into a Tudor mansion befitting his rank. Sir John was a favourite of the king and had been made High Sheriff of Essex (as well as Chancellor of the Duchy of Lancaster). In later years, however, he made the mistake of following the cause of Lady Jane Grey and was beheaded for treason as a result.

Layer Marney Church with, below, the impressive monument to the First Lord Marley found within. The First Lord Marley is said to haunt both the church and the impressive Tower next door. Both photos © James Parker

Beeleigh Abbey is possessed of what is known as a 'cyclic' ghost, one that manifests at certain times of the year. The phenomenon is an eerie crying and sobbing which is heard in a wing of the house on just one day, August 11. It is thought to be the voice of Sir John Gate, bewailing his upcoming fate on the block. According to one source, Sir John's headless ghost is seen on the precise anniversary of his execution (August 22), in a chamber known as the James Room. Another weird phenomenon has been reported from this room: sometimes the distinct outline of a human figure is found to be impressed into the mattress on the bed, even when the room has been kept locked for some days. Ghostly monks have also been seen at Beeleigh Abbey.

Another country house that started life as a monastery is Colne Priory at **Earls Colne**. In the 17th century, the resident Harlakenden family were disturbed by the sound of a tolling bell; the ghost, perhaps, of one in use in the days before the Dissolution when the priory was still a house of worship. In a letter from a friend of the family dated July 17, 1691, we learn:

'Off from the House was a Tomb-House, with a Chamber over it; his [Mr Harlakenden's] Butler, Robert Crow, and William, his Coach-man, used to lie in the Room. At Two of the Clock in the Morning there was always the sound of a great Bell tolling: They affirming it so, Mr Harlakenden slept in the Evening, so as to be awaked at One of the Clock, and lay betwixt his two Servants to satisfie himself. At Two of the Clock comes the usual Sound of a great Bell tolling, which put him into a Fright and Sweat.'

Subsequently several ministers and other pious individuals held a prayer meeting in the Tomb-House to 'cast out the Devil' and the spooky tolling was never heard again.

According to researcher Antony Hippisley-Coxe, a ghostly light has been seen in the Church of the Holy Cross at Waltham Abbey. Those who witness it are 'filled with a sense of evil'. Shutterstock/ c.byatt-norman

Priory Park in **Southend** has been created around the grounds and all that remains of Prittlewell Priory, founded in the 12ᵗʰ century by the Cluniac order. All that remains of the building is Refectory with a later brick building attached. However, one of the two authors of *Paranormal Essex* (unfortunately they omit to say which one) had a weird experience in which he apparently saw more of the Priory than has been visible for hundreds of years.

David Scanlan or Paul Robins (whichever one it was) visited the park many years ago with a friend and they followed a wall round its perimeter in order to get to the fountains and gardens within it. Later they started to head back the way they had come only to find the solid stone wall was no longer present. A short length of masonry ended in rubble but the long line of wall they had assiduously followed only a short time before was nowhere to be seen. Phantom monks and ladies in white are the more usual ghosts reported from Priory Park.

A phantom pirate haunts St Michael's Church, **Fobbing**. At least that's according to a local legend collected by Carmel King for her book, *Haunted Essex*. Because of his wicked ways, the pirate (a Frenchman, apparently), was banned from being buried in the churchyard so his grave was dug up against the wall, just outside the holy ground. It was said the grave would glow at night and that the pirate, annoyed perhaps that he had been denied a truly sanctified burial, was seen gazing sadly down at his weirdly illuminated last resting place.

Another tradition states that if anyone should be inclined to run round All Saint's Church in **Chelmsford** (at midnight no doubt and probably anti-clockwise), a spectral nun will appear and chase after them! Similar traditions apply to many different places in the UK, and not just churches, but why anyone should go to all that trouble to conjure up an angry spook is beyond me.

A much gentler holy woman is associated with the village named after her: **St Osyth**. St Osyth's Priory (more properly Abbey), was founded by the Augustinians in 1121. It survived until the Dissolution of the Monasteries, when the Prior and the monks were kicked out and the buildings given to Thomas Cromwell. The oldest and most striking remnant of the original structure is its 15th century gatehouse, a splendid example of decorative flint work. St Osyth was the daughter of a local Saxon king. Legend states she was beheaded by pagan Danish invaders but then calmly picked up her severed head and carried it to a nearby nunnery. Here she collapsed and a spring burst from the soil where she had fallen.

The headless ghost of St Osyth is said to be seen in the Priory grounds, in the vicinity of a well which some believe to be the site of the spring magically produced by her martyrdom. Elsewhere in the grounds, a ghostly monk has also been encountered.

The striking gatehouse of St Osyth's Priory. The Priory is haunted by Essex's holiest ghost. © James Parker

HAUNTED FORTRESSES

Colchester Castle is one of the oldest and most interesting in Britain. Building work began a few years after the Norman Conquest of 1066, on the site of a Roman temple to the Emperor Claudius. Material from this temple and the remains of the Roman town of Camelodunum were incorporated into its construction. Colchester Castle is not only ancient, it is massive, too. The castle's keep is half again the size of the Tower of London and is the largest surviving example in Europe.

The site has seen a lot of history. The Roman temple was razed to the ground by Boudicca (also known as Boadicea) during the revolt of the Iceni tribe which saw the massacre of the citizens of Cameludonum and later of Londinium. In the 13th century the castle was laid siege to by King John during his strife with rebellious nobles (leading finally to the signing of the Magna Carta). By the 17th century Colchester Castle was being used as a prison. In the 1640s the self-styled Witchfinder General Matthew Hopkins carried out his barbarous and phoney trials on hundreds of innocent people. In the same decade, during the English Civil War, two Royalist leaders, Sir Charles Lucas and Sir George Lisle, were executed to the rear of the castle. For years, no grass would grow on the spot where the two men were killed; a testament, it was said, to their innocence.

In the 1650s a Quaker, James Parnell, was fined £40 because the authorities disapproved of his religious preaching. He refused to pay and he was imprisoned at Colchester Castle. Tragically, in 1656, he died here. One version of events states that he was forced to climb a rope three times a day in order to get food from the gaoler and he either died of exhaustion and despair or fell to his death during this humiliating procedure. Parnell's ghost is now said to haunt the dungeon where he died.

The ghost of Colchester Castle dates from the time when it was being used as a prison. Shutterstock/ Brigida Soriano

For a long time the castle perched on a mound south of the village of **Hadleigh** had a reputation for being 'full o' ghosts'. The castle guards the Thames estuary and was begun in about the year 1215. It was greatly improved by Edward III in the 1360s to provide him with a handy retreat close to London. Unfortunately, the castle mound is composed of soft London clay which has led to considerable subsidence over the years. One of the towers now leans at a crazy angle. The abandoned castle was robbed of much of its stone and it is now very much a ruin.

In previous centuries mysterious lights were seen emanating from Hadleigh Castle but it has been suggested that these may have been smugglers' lanterns rather than ghosts. Local residents shunned the place after dark. Disturbing smugglers going about their nefarious business would have been a lot more dangerous than encountering a ghost, one would have thought. But not necessarily. The phantom of Hadleigh Castle is a woman dressed in white and known, straightforwardly enough, as the White Lady. White Ladies are traditional British ghosts. They often haunt castles, drifting mournfully about their battlements, as harmless a variety of spook as one could wish for. The White Lady of Hadleigh Castle, however, had a bit of a temper on her.

On one occasion, the White Lady accosted a passing milkmaid called Sally and commanded her to come to the castle at midnight. The startled Sally promised to do so but as day gave way to night, her fear of the ghost grew and she decided to stay away. The next day the angry phantom sought her out. To punish her for breaking her promise, the White Lady gave Sally a clout round the ear so severe that it dislocated her neck. Poor Sally never really recovered and was known as 'Wry-Neck Sal' ever after.

During the mid-19th century, Hadleigh Castle was also notorious for being the home of one 'Cunning Murrell'. James Murrell lived in a shack on the slope below the castle, from which he dispensed horoscopes, herbal remedies and spells, in the same manner as George Pickingill (see Canewdon in the previous chapter). Cunning Murrell was greatly respected during his lifetime and the locals were full

Hadleigh Castle is haunted by a Cunning Man and a
bad-tempered woman. Shutterstock/ Greg Benz

of stories of his exploits long after his death in 1860. His fame grew posthumously after Victorian writer Arthur Morrison, who liked to holiday in this part of Essex, discovered that a chest containing all of Murrell's papers still survived and had been unopened since his decease. Morrison got permission to open the box and what he found there, together with what he subsequently learned about Cunning Murrell, inspired him to write a book about him, which was published in 1900.

So famous – or infamous – was Cunning Murrell that rumours spread that he had not quite quit this mortal plane and that his ghost was still to be seen, wandering the castle mound and the nearby heath. His apparition seemed to be stooping and looking for herbs just as he had done in life.

The massive coastal defences of Coalhouse Fort at **East Tilbury** in the most part date from the 19th century, although a medieval armoury existed here five hundred years before. The Fort continued to defend London from incursion via the Thames throughout the two world wars. It then became a research centre before being decommissioned and sold to the local council in 1962. Since the early 1980s the Fort has been looked after by a voluntary organisation, who have set about restoring the buildings and opening them up to the public. In the twenty-year interval rumours abounded that Coalhouse Fort was regularly being broken into and used for black magic rituals. 'Satanic graffiti' was found scrawled on the walls.

The ghost of Coalhouse Fort is said to be that of a young woman, known as Beth. She is described as wearing a blue dress and having a come-hither look about her. Sometimes she is heard to giggle, sometimes sigh. An encounter with Beth apparently took place when David Scanlan, co-author of *Paranormal Essex*, was present. He and a team of paranormal investigators heard footsteps approaching them in tunnels near the entrance. They all shone their torches in the direction of the footsteps, which continued to approach them despite the fact that no one was to be seen. Then they stopped and an audible sigh was heard.

Mr Scanlan also recounts two more of his own spooky experiences at Coalhouse Fort, both of which took place in Room 24. On the first occasion he was startled to see what he believed to be the ghost of a '1940s soldier'. He writes: 'The figure looked round at me, bending slightly with his lower

The massive walls of Coalhouse Fort hide some spooky secrets.
Shutterstock/ S.m.u.d.g.e

half hidden in the doorway. I could clearly see the outline in the torchlight. It was so clear that I was able to identify the uniform as one typically worn in the 1940s by privates and NCOs.'

On the subsequent occasion, a medium was just starting to announce apparent contact with a spirit when a strong and entirely inexplicable gust of wind blew in from the tunnels. At the same time, the temperature dropped dramatically. The latter was not just felt, but registered on thermometers. Ghost hunts are frequently held at Coalhouse Fort. Its website states that although it cannot be guaranteed that visitors will experience anything supernatural, 'so far the Fort has not failed to provide us with extraordinary nights', and that 'whatever you experience will be 100% real'.

In the north of Essex, there is another fort with a haunted reputation. This is the Redoubt built during the Napoleonic wars to protect **Harwich** and the Suffolk town of Felixstowe over the water. In common with Coalhouse Fort, the Harwich Redoubt is also run by a voluntary group and it too hosts ghost hunts. It is supposedly haunted by a soldier who literally lost his head. The poor fellow became involved in a nasty accident in which his neck became caught up in a length of rope being used to hoist a heavy gun up to the battery.

One more fortification remains to be discussed and it's a very ancient one. Ambresbury Banks forms part of a chain of Iron Age hill forts built by Celtic tribes before the Roman invasion of Britain. It is now overgrown by trees in **Epping Forest** but the steep sides of its ramparts are still easy to distinguish. Ambresbury Banks is one of the many places offered up as the site of Queen Boudicca's last stand against

The apparition of Boudicca, Queen of the Iceni, is said to haunt an Iron Age hill fort in Epping Forest. (This statue of the warrior queen can be found on Westminster Bridge in London).

iStock

the might of Rome in AD61 (see Colchester, above). There is no evidence to support this assertion, unless it's the ghost of Boudicca herself, which is said to be seen wandering among the trees, bitterly regretting her defeat.

TWO ANCIENT TOWNS

Saffron Walden in the Uttlesford region of Essex gets its name from the long-defunct abbey of Walden and for the fact that centuries ago one of its most important industries was the growing of saffron. This costly yellow spice is extracted from the flowers of a kind of crocus and is still worth more than its weight in gold. In the medieval period, most of Saffron Walden's money came from wool, which is true of many of the county's towns and villages.

Saffron Walden's former wealth and importance is apparent from its majestic church, half-timbered Guildhall and the many grandly beautiful former medieval merchants' houses which line its streets. It is certainly one of Essex's most picturesque towns. There is a windmill, two rows of early medieval almshouses and many of its houses are painted in a variety of cheerful colours. Even the all-too-regular intrusion of jet planes coming into land at nearby Stansted airport fail to spoil the timeless charm of the place.

Saffron Walden boasts a number of haunted buildings. The six-centuries-old Maltings has a haunted cellar. When David Scanlan and Paul Robins took part in a paranormal investigation here in 2004 they heard loud and entirely inexplicable bangs and glimpsed 'shadowy movements' around them. The Maltings has now been converted into a residential property but in its former life, a man using a pulley to haul bags of malt up to the top floor tripped and fell to his death onto the cellar floor below. The authors believe it might be his ghost now haunting the cellar.

The ghost of the Elizabethan Cross Keys Hotel also manifests as strange noises, more specifically 'heavy, slow, ponderous footsteps'. They've not been heard for a while, but at one time the tread of the invisible spook would regularly be heard pacing the upper floor between 11pm and midnight on nights in the Christmas season. One witness, describing the experience to James Wentworth Day, related: 'The incident occurred at exactly midnight on Christmas Eve. I had just begun shutting the door to the side entrance, when I heard heavy footsteps above me. They were so heavy as to make the ceiling creak. My son rushed up the stairs to see if there was an intruder there. He came down very shortly, having examined the flat and the bedrooms and told me there was nobody.'

The ghost is said to be that of a soldier who guarded Royalist prisoners here during the turbulent days of the English Civil War, although why he remains on guard duty is unknown. The old Sun Inn has now been converted into a suite of offices. It too is haunted by a Cromwellian soldier, blamed for making noises after dark which resemble the dragging about of heavy furniture.

A quieter ghost haunts Hill House in the High Street: a maid-servant called Nelly Ketteridge who collapsed and died in a blizzard while trying to make her way home to Eldom on one of her days off in 1845. Her pathetic little ghost drifts down the passageways, a draught of freezing air following in her wake.

Saffron Walden is celebrated for its old world charm and harbours a number of ghosts. Shutterstock/ Tamara Kulikova

Coggeshall is another extraordinarily 'olde worlde' market town chock-full of medieval buildings. With a distinctive clock tower and wonky old houses and inns lining its streets, Coggeshall is also home to Paycocke's House, a wonderfully preserved medieval merchant's house now in the care of the National Trust. Rather disappointingly, Paycocke's seems to be ghost free, despite its great age and atmosphere. Indeed the town as a whole fails to get a mention in many ghost books on the subject.

Peter Underwood carried out some personal investigations at Coggeshall and outlined his results in his *Gazetteer of British Ghosts*. First up we have the Guild House, Market End. Here a mysterious light has been seen, shining from an attic room. In the same small room occupants often reported the sensation that they were not alone and indeed on occasions the ghost of a 'little man' has appeared at the foot of a bed. There was an important abbey at Coggeshall, so ghostly monks should be no surprise. They turn up at Cradle House, near Marshall Old Rectory, clad in white habits. They make their way into the garden and then do a little dance. Phantom monks are a dull set of spooks as a rule, so this behaviour is most unusual.

In the 1960s a house in Church Street gained a particular reputation for ghosts after building work was completed (bashing about an old property sometimes brings ghosts out of the woodwork). The then owners, the Grants, told of many 'curious happenings' in their home after they discovered a hidden room during the remodelling. A door set up between this space and a morning room began to be opened and closed by some invisible agency as soon as it was

Haunted Coggeshall is a pleasing mix of medieval, Georgian and early Victorian architecture.

fixed. A door into the kitchen behaved in a similar manner. Underwood further explains: 'Curious smells, the unexplained appearance of objects, a sudden sensation of coldness, footsteps and the feeling that a "presence" is in the house have all been reported by the Grants.' In addition an 'eerie mist' was seen near the staircase. None of this activity seems to have unduly unnerved the Grants and it may be supposed that the ghost or ghosts have settled down by now, as they so often do – until that is further building work is one day undertaken there.

THREE SPOOKY ISLANDS

Mersea Island is the UK's most easterly inhabited island. Situated between the estuaries of the rivers Blackwater and Colne and separated from the mainland by the Pyefleet Channel, Mersea is seven square miles of marsh and dotted farms and hamlets, with just one village of any substance, at West Mersea. Like most islands, it enjoys a special atmosphere all its own, remote from the bustle of the mainland.

A short causeway connects Mersea with the mainland. It is called The Strood and is the location of one of Essex's most famous ghosts. In 1926, local author James Wentworth Day first learnt of the ghost patrolling the Strood from an elderly ex-landlady of the five-hundred-year-old Peldon Rose Inn in nearby Peldon. He published Jane Pullen's encounter with the ghost in his 1954 book *Ghosts and Witches*.

'He came down off the Barrow Hill,' Mrs Pullen told Wentworth Day, referring to a Romano-British burial mound about a mile from where the Strood joins Mersea Island. 'The steady tramp of a man's feet, like it was a soldier marching, and he caught up with me and he walked all the way down to the Strood.

'I could see no one, yet the feet were close beside me, as near as I could have touched him. I walked down the road till I came on a man I knew. He was all a-tremble. He shook like a leaf. "I can hear him," he said, "but where is he? I can't see anyone." "Keep all along of me," I said to the man, "and no harm will come to you. 'Tis only one of those old Romans come out of the barrows to take his walk."

'And we walked on, sir, with the footsteps close beside us till we turned up a lane and he went on.'

This is only the first of a raft of encounters with the ghost of the Strood, commonly referred to as 'the Centurion'. Mrs Pullen's grandson was another witness. He was camping on Ray Island (now a nature reserve), which lies just off the Strood. He heard footsteps approaching him across the salt marsh but no one was visible in the bright moonlight.

'My grandson left his tent and ran home like a scared little boy,' Mrs Pullen told Wentworth Day, proud of her

The causeway connecting the mainland with Mersea Island is known as the Strood and is said to be the haunt of a Roman centurion. The fence alongside the road can be seen to the left of the photo. © James Parker

contrasting courage on meeting with the Centurion. Nearly twenty years later, Wentworth Day tracked down and interviewed Ivan Pullen about his experience on Ray Island for his book specifically on *Essex Ghosts*.

Mr Pullen told him: 'The moon shone bright as day. You could see from one end of the island to the other. The tide was coming in soft as silk. I was just turning over to go to sleep when I heard footsteps coming along the track from the saltings. You could hear his boots going squish-squash in the wet places. Then the footsteps came right up to the tent.

They stopped for a minute as though someone was listening … then, although the entrance flaps to the tent were tightly laced up, the footsteps came right into the tent. They made the ground shake within an inch or two of my nose where I lay. Then the footsteps walked out of the tent – although it was tightly laced.

'I was that scared I shook. Then I pulled myself together, grabbed my gun, undid the flaps, stepped out of the tent and looked round. You could see everything as plain as daylight. There was not a man in sight.'

On this further evidence that his unwelcome visitor had been not of this world, Mr Pullen went 'cold with fright'. I for one cannot blame him for haring off home.

A legend that the aforementioned Barrow Hill actually contains the burial of a Viking, rather than a Roman, is first to be found in a novel by the Victorian author Sabine Baring-Gould. The novel, *Mehalah*, is set in and around Mersea Island. In it Baring-Gould refers to a 'tradition' that two rival

Danish princes, twin brothers, are buried within it, still holding their swords and that on the nights of the new moon 'the flesh grows on their bones, and the blood staunches, and the wounds close, and the breath comes back behind their ribs'. When the moon is full, 'you can hear the brothers fighting below in the heart of the barrow'.

Mehalah was a best-seller but Baring-Gould later admitted to making up the legend of the rival Vikings. Any suspicions that the ghost of the Strood is anything other than a Roman soldier, however, are scotched by more recent reports in which the ghost is actually seen. An early sighting took place in 1970 when two Naval ratings were driving over the Strood on a misty night. A figure suddenly loomed out of the mist. They both saw clearly the distinctive outline of his Roman helmet, complete with cheek guards. The driver slammed on the brakes but the car passed straight through the apparition. They stopped but found the road empty. Neither of them were locals and they had never heard of the Centurion's ghost.

When former *Tomorrow's World* presenter William Woollard produced a series on the subject of the supernatural in 1996 (*Ghosthunters*), he interviewed numerous residents who had personally encountered the Centurion on the Strood, some more than once. According to Baring-Gould, ghostly Roman legionaries have also been seen at East Mersea and on other occasions the sound of fierce fighting, the clashing of swords and the yells of men, have been heard: an echo, he believed, of an early invasion of the Romans onto our shores. Baring-Gould was, for a time, rector at East Mersea and although his tale of the undead Viking princes is pure fiction, this latter nugget of information may well be based on the genuine experience of the local people.

An atmospheric shot of East Mersea. According to its former rector, Sabine Baring-Gould, the ghostly sounds of battle could be heard at East Mersea.
Shutterstock/ jayfish

Another ancient ghost is claimed for **Canvey Island**. This is not Roman, however, but Viking. Once again we are indebted to J Wentworth Day for the 'discovery' of this spook. An old wildfowler called Charlie Stamp related his experience while they were warming themselves one night in his hut overlooking the Benfleet Wall.

'I laid in me truckle bed lookin' out o' the winder of a midnight,' said Mr Stamp, 'Bright moon that was, bright as day. An' I reckon I had a dream. I dreamt there was an owd feller come up over the saltin's, over the wall an' across the plank into my garden. A rum owd feller. He stood six foot. He had a leather jerkin on wi' a belt an' a sword and cross-

57

garters below his knees. He had a funny owd hat on his head
– like a helm that was, with wings on. An' long moustaches
an' a beard.

"I've lost me ship, mate," he say. "I want to get a ship back
to me own country. I'm a lost man."

"Goo you up to Grays or Tilbury," I says. "You'll get a ship
there, mate, to carry you to any port in the world."

'He wagged his owd head an' he looked at me right
sorrowful. "I count I 'on't find no ship to take me to my port.
I'm a lost man."

'An' he walked over that sea-wall, master, an' away out on
the marsh, an' I never seed him no more.'

A dream it may have been but Wentworth Day was
particularly struck by the fact that the uneducated Mr Stamp,
who could neither read nor write, 'had never seen a picture
of a Viking warrior in his life'. Nor did he know that in
894AD, seven Viking longboats ravaged the coastline here,
until their crews were wiped out by a Saxon army. Whatever
the truth of Mr Stamp's vision, his Viking has now firmly
entered local ghost-lore and numerous books now refer to
the ghost of the 'owd' Dane as an established haunting. Betty
Puttick, in her *Ghosts of Essex*, for example, refers to 'the
famous Viking who stalks the saltings'.

Canvey Island's more frequently seen ghost is that of a Dutch
merchant. He wears old-fashioned clothes possibly dating
from the 1600s and carries a great bag of merchandise over
his shoulder. He is thought to have been murdered for his
goods. He haunts the marshy areas along the shores of the

island, away from the built-up centre. Carmel King's *Haunted Essex* adds two more ghosts to the list. One is of a woman who drowned in Canvey Island's lake, the other of a nun, who has been seen walking across a field, descending into the earth as if on an escalator as she does so.

Wallasea Island formerly possessed a farm called Duval's House, whose eerie reputation led to it being known to the islanders as Devil's House. Of this lonely place, a resident stated how: 'Some nights the cattle in the stock-yards seem to go mad. They stampede about as if the devil was after them. One night they broke through the fence and were all over the island in the morning. My old chap said that the devil was there himself, stirring them up with his fork!'

A view along the sea wall on Canvey Island. A ghostly Viking is said to be seen clambering over the wall in search of his ship.
Shutterstock/ Sue Chillingworth

Betty Puttick has recorded a tradition that Devil's House was haunted by the familiar spirit of a notorious witch called Mother Redcap. Perhaps this was the horrible, horn-headed thing said to sometimes peer in through the windows at midnight.

One room in Devil's House had the habit of becoming fearfully and inexplicably cold, a sensation accompanied by one of extreme dread. At the same time, a sound like great wings would be heard flapping around the ceiling. This happened so often that the room was kept locked. During the First World War, the room was opened up again for an officer who was too proud to bunk down with the men under his command in the barn. The morning after his first night in the house, he was found sleeping outside on the landing. His only explanation for this strange behavior was that the bed had been too soft! He left without having any breakfast and did not sleep there again.

Another account tells of a labourer who was pulled out of his bed by some invisible force and dragged down the stairs. But perhaps the most chilling story of Devil's Farm is the one set down by author Eric Maple, in his *The Realm of Ghosts*. Maple recounts the experience of another farm worker who had a terrifying experience in the barn. As the man passed by the building, he heard a voice calling his name and he felt compelled to go in. He then grew faint and felt oddly disassociated from reality. As if in a dream the labourer found himself gathering up a length of rope and tying one end in a noose round his neck. He threw the other end over a beam in the barn's roof. All the while he heard a sinister voice in his ear, insistently whispering: 'Do it, do it!'

The urge to hang himself seemed irresistible. Then he saw, perched on the beam, a hideous creature, ape-like with black fur and malevolent yellow eyes. Seeing it broke the spell and the man yanked the noose over his head and ran out of the barn. Was this a sighting of Mother Redcap's fiendish familiar?

The devastating flood of 1953, which destroyed so many homes and businesses, also washed away Devil's House Farm and nothing now remains of it. Perhaps this is just as well.

SURPRISING HAUNTS

Alongside the traditional haunted houses and castles there are a number of more unusual locations possessed of a ghost or two. One of these is the decommissioned nuclear bunker near **Braintree**. Kelvedon Hatch Nuclear Bunker is one of England's more unorthodox tourist attractions. Built in 1952 as an RAF station, it was later fitted with massive blast doors and anti-radioactive linings in order to house an emergency government in the event of a nuclear attack. Kelvedon Hatch Nuclear Bunker provides a fascinating if chilling insight into the tensions of the Cold War and the desperate mindset of those who would have hoped to not only survive but also govern after a nuclear holocaust (not that there would have been much left to govern!).

Perhaps the most surprising aspect of Kelvedon Hatch Nuclear Bunker is that it should be considered haunted. Although it was designed to accommodate six-hundred personnel, it was (thankfully) never used and only a skeleton staff would ever have been employed here. Nonetheless, paranormal investigations have become frequent events at the bunker, often used to raise money for charity. Those who have taken part have experienced sudden drops in temperature, heard subdued voices in rooms found to be empty and being creeped out by a general sense of the place being somehow crowded with people they cannot see. It is possible this ghostliness dates from the time of its original use by the RAF or subsequent brief life in the early 1960s as a civil defence centre.

Equally unusual was the haunted oil refinery at **Coryton**. The refinery was later converted to a power station and the site, which today forms part of the Port of London, is now under development. The ghost of a former worker was seen near a separator unit. In his book *Our Haunted Kingdom*, Andrew Green reports a sighting by employee George Poole. Mr Poole was sitting in the cab of a vehicle near a filtration unit one evening when he heard footsteps approaching.

'The footsteps moved nearer,' writes Green, 'and he saw, in the glare from one of the standard road lamps, the figure of a stout man, 5ft 9in tall, wearing a boiler suit and a white steel helmet. The man continued to walk on beside "the moat" (the gulley surrounding certain equipment sites) until he was only seven yards from George. Mr Poole, jumping out from the vehicle, began to run towards the figure, calling out as he moved. As the figure reached a crossroad it "just vanished".'

The apparition was seen by a number of different witnesses and was thought to be of a worker who suffered a fatal accident when he fell into a tank of oily water and drowned.

Not far away is **Southend-on-Sea**. Southend Pier has had a rather chequered history, with a number of bad fires dramatically changing its appearance over the years. For decades the grand Pavilion was one of the top destinations on the south coast but it was destroyed by fire in 1959. Another devastating blaze occurred in 1976 and then, just after major refurbishment work had been completed, a ship crashed into the Pier, undoing all the good work. In 1995 the bowling alley which had replaced the Pavilion burnt down. Despite all this drama, Southend Pier has survived and is still a popular tourist attraction.

Southend Pier is one of the more unusual haunted locations in Essex.
Copyright Liubov Terletska

An extraordinary incident apparently took place during a recent revamp of Southend Pier's entrance. A policeman spotted a man haring down the street and stopped him, suspicious that a crime may have been committed. The man turned out to be a builder employed on the Pier's makeover. He was clearly terrified. He told the astonished constable that he was running away from a ghost! He said he had been engaged on his work when, looking up, he realised he was being watched by something unearthly in 'old-fashioned clothes'. He was instantly filled with dread and simply ran away. Another ghost – or possibly the same one – has been seen at the opposite end of the Pier. A security guard chased it but it vanished in an area which at the time of the sighting had remained damaged by one of the many fires to have plagued the Pier.

Continuing the theme of unusual haunted locations, we must consider the handsome Jacobean-style Victorian railway station at **Maldon**. Maldon East & Heybridge Railway Station (to give its full name) has long been disused, although the building had been running as a pub until recently. Since at least the 1950s, the station was known to be haunted. Numerous witnesses over a number of years encountered the ghostly figure of a woman in white on Platform 2. A station master's wife told newspaper reporters that she had seen the 'white-shrouded figure' glide up the path towards the waiting room. On each of the four occasions she saw it, the apparition was accompanied by an eerie groaning sound and a sudden drop in temperature.

The identity of the endlessly waiting woman is unknown. A builder helping to convert the station into a pub added an eerie extra to the story, however. He said: 'When we were pulling up the floorboards we found a mummy-shaped area of damp soil. Each time we tried to shift it, it resumed its spooky shape and the soil seemed damp to the touch.'

Wesley Downes tells a splendidly gruesome ghost story from **Clacton** in his *Memories of an Essex Ghosthunter*. His correspondent – who wished to remain anonymous – told him that late one night his dog, which had earlier run away while he was walking it along the beach, returned home and scratched at the door to be let in. This was not an unusual occurrence, for it often ran off, only to return with a rabbit or some other unfortunate small mammal in its mouth. On this occasion, however, it proudly held a human arm in its jaws! The arm ended at the elbow and had strands of seaweed attached to it. Not quite sure what to do with this grim relic from the sea, the dog's owner gingerly wrapped it

The pretty town of Maldon has a number of haunted locations, including its handsome old railway station. Shutterstock/ S.m.u.d.g.e

in polythene and deposited it in the freezer, intending to take it to the police station the following morning.

That night his house was disturbed by a series of ghastly moans and groans and an insistent rapping sound. No normal explanation could be found for the noises, which continued all night. The following morning the Clacton resident took the arm to the police station. Unfortunately, this didn't prevent the haunting. The moans, groans and thumps began again that night. It was as if the dog had brought something ghostly into the house along with the body part. It took a number of nights before the spirit, or whatever it was, quietened down and eventually quit the house.

Relics of a different sort, apparently linked to a woman who was executed as a witch, were found in the picture-postcard village of **Finchingfield** some years ago. Joan Forman viewed the objects in the 1970s at an early 17th century thatched cottage on the outskirts of the village. The owner, a Mr Pedder, showed the author of *Haunted East Anglia* a stick, somewhat longer than a walking stick, which he had found buried in the wall round his property. The wood was carved at each end with coiled serpents. Mr Pedder explained that it was a 'witch stick' used to beat suspected witches. A member of Mr Pedder's family who had lived in the cottage in the late 18th century had been beaten to death after she was caught apparently teaching spells to young girls in the village. He believed the stick was one of those used in the assault and may have been hidden in the wall as a protective charm.

No less interesting was a second stick, more elaborately carved with animals and believed to be a 'fertility stick', which was found hidden below the thatch on the top of the roof. This too had probably been concealed centuries ago as a good luck charm, perhaps to ward off any malign influences hanging around after the tragedy involving Mr Pedder's ancestress.

However, it was the two pewter mugs found in the back garden which attracted a supernatural presence. Mr Pedder had been carrying out a major overhaul of his garden when he turned his attention to the ground around one of several old apple trees. As he began to dig beneath the tree, he felt someone shove him in the back. Recovering his balance, he looked up angrily only to find that he was alone. The garden was empty. After a moment or two to collect his thoughts, he continued his work in another part of the garden but when he returned to his digging beneath the apple tree, the invisible presence pushed him again. Clearly something was trying to make him work elsewhere.

Determined not to be put off, Mr Pedder began to dig away with a will and soon uncovered the pair of pewter mugs mentioned above. They were of some age but rather plain and not of any great value. However, as Joan Forman points out, they may well have been worth a lot more to a poor cottager of the 18th century. Had they belonged to the unfortunate woman who, on seeing the mob come to her door, rushed out and buried these modest treasures so that they wouldn't fall into their hands? No doubt she had hoped to recover them herself later, not knowing the brutal and ultimately fatal treatment she was to suffer. Had her lingering spirit attempted to prevent their discovery one last time two centuries later?

Finchingfield, where several strange artifacts link to a tragedy and a possible ghostly presence at an old cottage. Shutterstock/ Gordon Bell

AN ANONYMOUS HAUNTED HOUSE

While compiling my website, Uncanny UK, I received a fascinating account of an Essex haunting. Although I have the name of the contributor on file, she wished to remain anonymous and was keen not to have the location identified to protect the people who now live in the house where they experienced so much weird activity. All I am permitted to tell you is that the house is a 1960s bungalow on the outskirts of a village, with a river at the bottom of the garden beyond which lie the remains of a medieval abbey. Despite the imposed anonymity, it struck me that the story – a summary of it, at least – was worth retelling, for it has never before been reproduced in print.

Initial indications there might be a ghostly presence in the house were fairly mild: taps turning themselves off and on for no apparent reason and the mysterious disappearance of objects, which would suddenly reappear in places where they could not have been overlooked before. When the dark nights of winter set in, 'bright balls of light' were seen floating round a maple tree in the garden. On a subsequent night the lights had made their way into the conservatory and were then seen 'shooting up and down the hall'. Another oddity was that for three summers running, on almost the same date, their bathroom was found to be inexplicably filled with a swarm of bright green grasshoppers.

The dog developed the unnerving habit of raising his hackles and growling at empty corners of the room. Strange thumps and bangs disturbed their rest at night.

'Sitting watching telly one night we got our first real taste of things to come,' writes my correspondent. 'Out of nowhere we got soaking wet! It was as though a bucket full of water was tipped over our heads. Obviously we shrieked and jumped up, but the ceiling was completely dry. Everything was, apart from us.

'The dark shadows appeared next: fleeting glimpses from the corner of your eye but when you turned nothing would be there. This was not an occasional occurrence, it was all the time. The atmosphere in the house became very heavy. It felt as though there was a constant loud party going on that we couldn't hear and that we weren't invited to.'

With a baby on the way, these disturbances were insufficient to drive the young couple from their home. After the child's birth, the young mum began to experience persistent nightmares of 'being stalked by an unknown predator'. Even during the day she would be plagued by the feeling that something was trying to get into the house. She put the phobia down to post-baby hormones.

Four years later, her husband was walking their dog, accompanied by their young daughter, when he was terrified by the sight of what he described as a black panther, lying in a patch of sunshine by the river. He could hardly believe his own eyes. But when, a few weeks later, he heard growling behind the hedge near their child's play equipment, he took no chances and called in the police. They confirmed that 'there had been a few reports' and blandly informed the couple that they should 'move the play equipment closer to the house as children playing and screaming sound like an animal in distress and would attract a big cat for food'! The cat, if it ever truly existed, was never seen or heard of again.

Finding a black panther near the bottom of their garden was just one of the many strange things to occur in and around a humble 1960s bungalow in an Essex village. Shutterstock/ Eric Isselee

Things got even weirder. My correspondent explained: 'My husband would take the dog out for a walk across the fields surrounding our house late at night. On one occasion his torch batteries had failed and he had fallen down a ditch and arrived home covered in mud and stinging nettle blisters. There was no mobile phone coverage in the area so I bought a pair of walkie-talkies just in case he came a cropper again and then he could call me for help.

'On returning one evening he entered the conservatory where I was sitting and we were just chatting normally. Both handsets were still switched on: he was holding one and the other was next to me on the sofa. Then out of just one of the handsets (my husband's) came a most despicable voice. It was that of an old man. It made your skin crawl and made me want to be sick. All it said was: "I died and now I'm dead."

'How could a signal be received through just one handset when both were tuned to the same frequency? And that voice was beyond chilling. It was not human. I really cannot describe the total repulsion it made us feel.'

Enough was enough. They decided to sell the house. One further spooky experience was to occur, however. On the night they visited the estate agents, my correspondent woke up with the feeling that someone was standing outside her bedroom door. At first she thought it might be her little girl but when she opened the door she saw 'a man as solid as you or I' standing between her daughter's bedroom and her own. 'He had a dark suit and waistcoat, a fob watch and a hat on. The only giveaway that he wasn't from this world was the fact that his hat didn't seem to be quite finished at the top and there were bright lights zooming around the top of it as if like a vortex.'

She screamed, rousing her husband, who also saw the apparition. They stared at it for a while in disbelief.

'We both felt no fear,' writes my correspondent, 'and my husband said to just ignore him and shut our eyes, say a prayer and go to sleep, and to my surprise afterwards we both did just that.'

Sometime later, she described the ghost to her mum, who was convinced that it must have been her own grandfather (ie my correspondent's great-grandfather). On being shown a photo of him, she (and her husband) felt convinced that it was indeed his ghost they had seen. Her great-grandfather, if that is who it was, may have manifested again. After a number of disappointments over the sale of the house, when she was feeling really down, she heard a calming voice tell her, 'You will move on the 28th of August.' That turned out to be the date they did finally quit the haunted bungalow. Their new home (so far!) has been ghost free.

HOUNDS FROM HELL

One of the strangest yet most widespread forms of apparition in the British Isles is the so-called Black Dog. The classic Black Dog description is a huge black hound of the mastiff variety but with a shaggy pelt and fiery eyes. The size is commonly stated as being similar to that of a calf.

Not all Black Dogs are black, not all are huge, not all have shaggy fur or glowing eyes, but they all have certain characteristics in common: they are more or less canine and they haunt lonely lanes at night or twilight. Black Dogs have been seen for centuries in all parts of Britain (and indeed the world) and have gone under a variety of regional names, such as Padfoot, Trash, Shriker and Gwyllgi. They have a very unpleasant habit of following solitary travellers, keeping abreast of them or pacing along unnervingly behind. They

Arthur Conan Doyle's Hound of the Baskervilles is arguably Britain's best-known Black Dog. Although the hound in the Sherlock Holmes yarn turns out to be a living animal, the story was inspired by legends regarding the supernatural variety.

have never been known to attack a person but in some areas they are considered death omens.

The origin of the Black Dog phenomenon is a mystery. Certainly they are not considered apparitions of once living dogs (although ghostly pet dogs occur, too). They are otherworldly, terrifying spectres – minor demons of the British countryside. I have personally received reports of Black Dogs seen as recently as the 1970s. Although they may seem archaic, figures to be found only in antiquated folklore, they are with us still.

In East Anglia the spectre is called Black Shuck, from an Anglo-Saxon word meaning 'devil'. This part of the world has long been considered the spiritual home of the Black Dog. This is partly because so many reports of its appearance have been collected and promoted by J Wentworth Day, the Essex author whose researches have already featured so strongly in the present volume. In his book of *Essex Ghosts* he writes:

'In the late 1930s, I rented the shooting of the Guisnes Court Estate at **Tolleshunt d'Arcy**, which included that wild, wet, roadless peninsula of Old Hall Marshes, one of the six best duck shoots in England. The gamekeeper was William Fell, who looked like a Viking. He knew the marshes backwards. He feared no man. Poachers were terrified of him. Yet he admitted that he had been frightened out of his life when one night he and another man were driving in a horse and trap from Peldon along the Wigborough Road to Guisnes Court.

'Suddenly, somewhere near the Salcott crossroads, an enormous black dog with drooping ears and a crimson, slavering tongue appeared. It was, said Fell; "As big as a calf, with eyes like bike lamps, and so tall that its head was level with the floorboards of the cart." It followed them for half a mile or so then suddenly disappeared.'

Wentworth Day also had first-hand testimony of another encounter with Black Shuck near **Tollesbury**. A young woman was cycling past the lane leading up to Gorwell Hall when she suddenly realised a huge hound was keeping pace with her. The girl had been sent to fetch a midwife and it was long after dark. The dog was as long as her bicycle and its head was level with her handlebars. She particularly noticed its 'harsh black coat … so rough and uncared-for'. It vanished at the junction of the lane but the girl encountered it again on the return journey. It was lying in the middle of the road. 'Its eyes were shut, but its huge tongue looked like bright red velvet,' she recalled. She managed to squeeze past the monster without waking it. When she got home, she alerted the household about the huge dog, concerned for the safety of the midwife who was following on. However, when her parents went to investigate, there was nothing to be seen. According to Betty Puttick, in 1960 another cyclist had a similar experience on the B1026 which runs alongside the **Blackwater Estuary**. Just as the daylight was fading, a Black Dog suddenly appeared alongside him. 'It seemed an unfriendly animal,' writes Puttick in her *Ghosts of Essex*, 'for it snapped and snarled as it ran, and after a while the man swerved his bicycle towards the dog and jumped down, hoping to drive it off. But as he looked around for his menacing companion, to his amazement he found he was alone. There was absolutely no sign of the dog, which had vanished into thin air, and he was uneasily conscious of a strange, oppressive atmosphere.'

The marshland around Tollesbury is one of the haunts of the terrifying Black Shuck. Shutterstock/ joingate

Another spectral hound is known to pad silently the lane between the church and the village of **Hockley**, near Rayleigh. Something similar, but somehow even more horrible, is known to patrol the B1052 between **Newmarket** and **Saffron Walden**. Although its body resembles the usual black, shaggy dog, its face is more ape-like than canine. On occasions it has been seen to shamble along on two legs. This unusual variant on the Black Dog has been given the name of the Shug Monkey.